Fresh-Brewed Life

Study Guide

Published by

Nelson
multi media group
a Thomas Nelson Company

A division of Thomas Nelson Publishers

Printed in the United States of America
ISBN 1-4185-3226-6

For Information
Call Thomas Nelson Publishers **1.800.251.4000**
www.thomasnelson.com

Introduction

"And the day came when the risk it took to remain tight in the bud was more painful than the risk it took to blossom." Anais Nin

When will you begin living the life you've always wanted to live? When things finally slow down? When you get married, or get the job you've wanted? When you move into your new house or when your husband finally gets that big promotion? When the kids leave for college? Almost every woman I know has a list of reasons that tempt her to wait on life, to postpone her passion, or to put joy on hold until some later time.

Well, take a deep breath and look at your calendar. Mark this day. Make a note of today and say a gentle yes to letting your life begin this very moment. Right now. No more delays. No more excuses. No more waiting on anybody else to do it for you, to get it right, to make you happy, or to finish their work. The time has come for you to tear up that mental list of tempting reasons and wake up to join your life already in progress.

I have written my book, Fresh-Brewed Life, as a journey in nine cups. In this small group study I will only deal with four of those cups. This doesn't mean you'll only wake up halfway—it simply means you have an opportunity to let God begin to stir your soul. I invite you to embark on this journey with your bible, a journal, and a small group that will be your companions along the trip.

Coffee is a wonderful metaphor for this study because it's so much more than a beverage, it's an invitation. Getting together for coffee is about spending time together and having good conversation. So even if you don't like coffee, this study still holds the same promise: wake up to a richer life.

I define a fresh-brewed life as a "surrendering to God the whole bean essence of who you are, allowing yourself to be finely ground, letting the fiery love of God pour over you, releasing from your life the most fragrant aroma possible."

This is your wake up call.

Nicole Johnson,
Easter 2000

Ten signs you know you need a wake-up call to a fresh-brewed life:

1. You yelled at your minister last Sunday, or ever.

2. You fell asleep at your own party.

3. You lobby for chocolate to be one of the four food groups.

4. Your husband doesn't want sex, and you're happy about that.

5. You called your best friend and started chatting, and she said, "Who is this?"

6. The people you work with are asking when your next vacation is.

7. Your kids look forward to going to school.

8. Your idea of a good time is a coma.

9. You can't remember your last vacation.

10. You agreed to serve God, but only in an advisory capacity.

Table of Contents

About the Author

Nicole Johnson is an actress, a television host, and a guest dramatist with the Women of Faith conferences. She has been traveling and performing for over ten years, delighting audiences across America with a lively blend of comedy and drama.

Fresh-Brewed Life

Cup Number One

Embrace Your Beauty

Reflection and Discussion

PSALM 57:8
Awake, my soul!

JOHN 10:10
I have come that they may have life, and that they may have it more abundantly.

Beauty Designed for One

What would it take for us to trust that the Lord has gently created each of us to be beautiful in our own way? Not one woman has been overlooked by his delicate gift.

Unfortunately for some women, beauty has become an enemy. Beauty, or the perceived lack of it, has been the cause of painful rejections, passed over promotions, struggles in marriage, or even self-hatred.

Where do most women you know get their images of beauty?

- ○ Family
- ○ Friends
- ○ Peers
- ○ Magazines
- ○ Advertising
- ○ Scripture

What about you?

_____

_____

_____

_____

"The most beautiful make-up of a woman is passion. But cosmetics are easier to buy."

Yves St. Laurent

We're scared to try to uncover the beauty within us. Isn't it better, we reason, to dismiss beauty than to try to embrace something that we fear we don't have? Won't we look foolish if we think we are beautiful when we are not?

All of these were my thoughts as I began to think about how negative I had become toward beauty. I was so afraid that I didn't have "it" that I rejected it before "it" or anyone could reject me.

Think about occasions in your own life when you were at odds with the world's ideals of beauty. What false responses should we avoid?

_____

_____

_____

_____

_____

_____

What I missed in this thinking was what a refusal to embrace beauty was doing to me and to my spirit, not to mention what it was doing to those around me.

The more I dismissed beauty as something that belonged to others, the more I rejected opportunities to nurture my own spirit. The more I held my physical appearance at arm's length and tried not to care about it, the more I died on the inside.

"The mass media often trivialize our lives and our achievements, narrowing the litmus test of female worth to one question: Does she have dimpled thighs or crow's feet? If so, onto the trash heap of history."

Susan Douglas

Does you agree that women are torn over how we see ourselves?

○ Yes
○ No
○ Maybe

If so, what does that do to us inside?

_____

_____

_____

_____

But God is calling us to life! On the inside first, and then on the outside! We can't focus on the outside alone. Because, there is no beauty in make-up. Expensive clothes will not make you beautiful.

The secret of beauty lies in being an alive, awake woman with something to offer the world—namely, yourself.

What negative voices do you hear in your life about how you look? (E.g., from your past, your family, our culture)

_____

_____

_____

What happens to us when we listen to such voices rather than God?

_____

_____

_____

_____

"I am beautiful to the one who loves me.' Or 'I will be loved if I am beautiful.' In the gap between those two statements, thousands of women live in fear and sorrow."

Karen Lee-Thorp and Cynthia Hicks, Why Beauty Matters

Beauty is:

* Less about your face, and more about your smile;
* Less about the shape of your eyebrows, and more about the light in your eyes;
* Less about the length of your legs, more about the bounce in your step.

As you participate in your life with a warm smile and a generous spirit, you can trust that you are beautiful.

What does is mean in practice to be "comfortable with who God made us to be?" To be God's "beloved"? To "embrace our beauty"?

_____

_____

_____

_____

In what ways might our lives change if we pressed deeper into such truths?

_____

_____

_____

_____

All my life I thought beauty was only what I looked life. Now I understand it's so much more than that.

True beauty cannot be separated into component parts. It is the total package that reveals someone's beauty, not one thing.

"If thigh reducing creams really work, why don't they make your hand smaller?"

Rita Rudner, Comedian

Living a fresh-brewed life brings out the beauty in us because it is revealing more of the authentic woman that God designed each of us to be.

How do we discover what Nicole calls "the secret of being an alive, passionate woman in this world"?

_____

_____

_____

_____

Wake up and embrace your beauty!

Action Point:

Are there women in your life—a daughter, a sister, a friend, a colleague—who need encouragement to discover the beauty God has given them? If so, list their names below.

_____

_____

_____

How will you share with them what you have learned here about real beauty?

_____

_____

_____

_____

"May you live all the days of your life."
Jonathan Swift

Percolations

Books
* *Why Beauty Matters*, Karen Lee-Thorp and Cynthia Hicks
* *The Good Life*, Ruth McGinnis
* *Fresh-Brewed Life: A Stirring Invitation to Wake Up Your Soul* (chapter 4)

Movies
* Babette's Feast
* My Fair Lady
* Beauty and the Beast

Music
* Storms, Nancy Griffith
* Carry Us Through, Sarah Masen

Fresh-Brewed Adventures

* Write a letter to your mother about her beauty.

* If you've never spent a day at a spa, go for it. Get a massage and a facial, maybe a manicure or a pedicure. Treat yourself to a kindness day.

* If you've done the spa day before, try a listening retreat, for your soul. Find a spiritual director, and spend half a day with God.

Directed Journaling

* Make two columns on your journal page. Write the names of your
family members who communicated to you that you had worth and
value. Underneath their names write some of the things they said that stand
out in your mind. Was there anyone who told you that you were beautiful?
Any special aunts or uncles or grandparents? Write their words in your journal.

* Now think through some of the negative messages you received. Who in your family
caused you to question your worth? Was there a sibling or parent that constantly
criticized your appearance? Was your father able to express his love to you? Write out
prayers of forgiveness.

* For most of us, the second side of the page will be a lot easier to fill in. No only do we
remember the negative far more than we do the positive, chances are good that there
wasn't as much positive.

Notes

_____

_____

_____

_____

_____

_____

_____

_____

_____

_____

_____

_____

_____

Fresh-Brewed Life

Cup Number Two

Listen to Your Longings

Reflection and Discussion

PSALM 63:1
O God, you are my God, I earnestly I seek you; my soul thirsts for you, my body longs for you, in a dry and weary land where there is no water.

PSALM 38:9
All my longings lie open before you, O Lord; my sighing is not hidden from you.

Listen to your Longings

Staring out the sliding glass door into the ocean, a strong sense of emptiness fills her heart. It is her last day of vacation. She doesn't hate her life or her job, yet the thought of returning to both causes great sadness. She'll be at her desk tomorrow, waiting another year for vacation. An ache sets in. She was made for more.

Patty wipes a tear as she hangs up the phone. It is always so hard to say goodbye. Her best friend lives ten hours away and the loneliness she feels is from more than just the miles separating them. They are soul mates and Patty yearns for more time together. They had just spent an hour on the phone and could easily have spent more. "What is wrong with me? Why can't I be grateful for the time we have instead of being depressed that we don't have more?" She can't muster up the gratitude, and she puts her head in her hands and weeps. She was made for more.

They have been married for fifteen years. They are still in love and deeply committed to each other. But they are different, and as much as she doesn't want to admit it, there are times when Caroline finds empty places in her soul that her husband can't reach. She tries not to think about it much, she stays really busy, but there are times when she feels like a complete stranger to him. "Does he really know me?" she wonders as she lays awake at night. The next morning as she washes her hair, she tries to send her feelings right down the drain with the shampoo. She was made for more.

"The hunger for status is simply a swollen manifestation of the God-given longing for respect."
Karen Lee-Thorp and Cynthia Hicks, *Why Beauty Matters*

Longings. Coming face to face with the fact that there are empty places in our lives that haven't been filled.

Yearnings. Wanting more than we have: more love, more enjoyment, more passion, more hope, more rest.

Cravings. The hope of finding something that will satisfy the rumbling we feel in the stomachs of our souls.

Longings can begin to surface after a number of years in the same job. Women begin to wonder, "Is this all there is?" The same awakening happens in a marriage when a woman realizes that she wants more love or tenderness than her husband can give. At the dinner table in the middle of supper, a hope for peace and a strong yearning for rest begin to rise up inside.

Nicole shared her sense of a void because of a "longing for a father." What is yours?

_____

_____

_____

_____

_____

The fact is you were made for more than this world has to offer you.

That's why we can have a marvelous vacation and it satisfies us deeply on one level and leaves us empty on another.

"Jealousy is an oddly wrapped gift that points the way toward where we want to go."
SARK

That's why we can receive praise and honor from other people, and yet feel insecure and alone at the same time. We were made to run on high-test fuel, and the best we get here is 89-grade octane. It's not that we are ungrateful or greedy. God has designed us to want more out of life, and we won't be satisfied until we get it.

List the big things that are genuine disappointments in your life.

_____

_____

_____

_____

_____

How have you reacted to them?

_____

_____

_____

_____

_____

If you are honest, has the net effect of the disappointments driven you away from God or brought you closer?

_____

_____

_____

_____

_____

"When at last I cling to you with all my being, for me there will be no more sorrow, no more toil. Then at last I shall be alive with true life, for my life will be wholly filled by you."

Saint Augustine

So, are longings one big cosmic set-up for frustration? Perhaps, if we only view them as something to be overcome or eradicated. If we spend all our time trying to get them "filled up."

But, if we lean in close and put our ears to the chests of our souls and listen to our longings, they can teach us to understand God and ourselves in a way that would not happen if we were permitted to have everything we longed for.

What happens to us when we fall for the false response to longings and become "spectators"? Will this free us from pain in our lives?

_____

_____

_____

_____

_____

What happens when we become hypercritical "evaluators"? Will this way of approaching disappointment lead us to more joy?

_____

_____

_____

_____

Though they're sometimes used interchangeably, wishes, dreams, and longings are distinctly separate. If we confuse them, we could find ourselves depressed very easily. Consider the examples on the following page:

"The tragedy of life is not in the fact of death, but in what dies inside us while we live."

Norman Cousins

Wishes	Dreams	Longings
A relationship	A husband	A perfect man
Some cash	More money	Enough money to solve all your problems
More time	An incredible vacation	A place of complete freedom and rest
To be thinner	To be a size four	To be Gwyneth Paltrow

Do you agree with Nicole's distinction between wishes, dreams, and longings?

O   Yes

O   No

O   Not sure

Do these categories accurately reflect what you know of yourself and others?

_____

_____

_____

What we don't have changes us far more than what we have. I believe we are made like swiss cheese, and the holes in us are actually supposed to be there. The holes themselves make us who we are and they remind us that there is more to this life, and we shouldn't just settle.

What does it mean to respond positively to "the holes that are supposed to be there"?

_____

_____

_____

"There are two sources of unhappiness in life. One is not getting what you want; the other is getting it."
George Bernard Shaw

17

How do we avoid "medicating our longings" and use them instead as "treasure maps" to help us discover what God has in store for us?

_____

_____

_____

_____

Wake up and listen to your longings!

Percolations

Books
* *Yearning: Living Between How It Is and How It Ought to Be*, Craig Barnes
* *The Unknown God: Searching for Spiritual Fulfillment*, Alister E. McGrath
* *Fresh-Brewed Life: A Stirring Invitation to Wake Up Your Soul* (chapter 3)

Movies
* City of Angels
* Trip to Bountiful
* The Horse Whisperer

Music
* Big Horizon, David Wilcox
* Flyer, Nancy Griffith
* Behind the Eyes, Amy Grant

Fresh-Brewed Adventures

* Write a letter to God, confiding in Him your deepest longings.
* Poetry is the language of longings. Write a poem about one particular longing.
* Take one hour this week and go on a date with yourself. Schedule it on your calendar. Bring your journal and your Bible, and go to your favorite coffee shop, sit on your deck, check out a new art store, or take a long, leisurely bath. Wherever you are, the goal is to create a space to be still and listen to your longings.

Directed Journaling

Who are you jealous of? Why?

What is someone else doing that you wish you were doing?

Write about two longings in your life.

What do you dream about?

Notes

_____

_____

_____

_____

_____

_____

_____

_____

_____

_____

_____

_____

_____

_____

_____

_____

_____

_____

Fresh-Brewed Life

Cup Number Three

Interview Your Anger

Reflection and Discussion

PSALM 4:4
Be angry, and do not sin.
Meditate within your heart on your bed, and be still.

EPHESIANS 4:26
"Be angry, and do not sin": do not let the sun go down on your wrath,

Interview Your Anger

I don't have a problem with Anger!

* Are you critical of other people?
* Are your friendships peppered with angry incidents?
* Are your kids constantly doing something wrong?
* Does your family frequently ask, "Mom, why are you mad?"
* Have you broken anything in anger?
* Does your husband feel praised by you?

Anger is so hard for women to admit. We are afraid of it. We don't want to be labeled angry. There is an ugly stigma attached to women who are angry. Men are considered powerful when they are angry. They are leaders, who might be seen as forceful or strong.

But women who are angry are often labeled shrews, nags, men-haters, irrational, or out of control. We even get called the ever-popular "b" word. So, we avoid it, and get angry silently.

"Anger repressed can poison a relationship surely as the cruelest words."
Dr. Joyce Brothers

We try to hide our anger. We take our hurt and frustration and bury it like a dog does a bone, creating holes and tunnels beneath every room in our house. When our husbands, or friends, sense some buried anger beneath the surface, they ask, "What's wrong?" "Nothing!" we snarl, as we slam things around.

Do you agree that women today are not allowed to be angry?

○ Yes
○ No
○ Not sure

If so, where do you see evidence of this?

_____

_____

_____

_____

How does it make you feel?

_____

_____

_____

_____

Why do you think we might be afraid of being perceived as angry?

_____

_____

_____

_____

"Anger is a tool for change when it challenges us to become more
of an expert on the self and less of an expert on others."
Harriet Goldhor Lerner

What would it mean if you were angry?

_____

_____

_____

_____

_____

I don't want to be mad, and if I am mad, I certainly don't want anyone labeling me that way. So I stuff, bury, hide, avoid, deny, close up and shut down (or think I do). And then, lo and behold, I find myself standing in front of my dryer in a rage because I can't find the mate of my black sock! Or I'm standing in the grocery store reduced to tears because there is no more Starbucks Ice-Cream. I have to ask myself, where is this coming from? Is this anger really about socks or ice-cream?

Think back on experiences of anger in your life. What triggered them and what do they show you about your situation and yourself?

_____

_____

_____

_____

_____

Real "ice-cream disappointment" is brief. "Sock anxiety" (even during PMS) is not filled with rage. When we find ourselves intensely angry over the little things, or things that should be little things, it's time to wake up. Anger is a signal to heed carefully. When the CHECK ENGINE SOON light comes on in your automobile, there's something you need to pay attention to. Tears in the grocery store are telling you something. Yelling at your children over Legos is your soul sending you a message: CHECK ENGINE SOON.

"Don't be afraid to take a big step if one is indicated. You can't cross a chasm in two small jumps."
David Lloyd George

In what ways do people often try to deny their anger but only end up expressing it in different forms, such as a critical spirit?

_____

_____

_____

_____

_____

Are there places in your life where you are mad at God? How are you handling them?

_____

_____

_____

_____

In order to raise the hood and find out why the warning light keeps coming on, I propose that we interview ourselves. "Where does it hurt? What happened?" Interview questions get to the heart of the matter.

Psychologists tell us that anger is made up of fear, frustrations and hurt. What might you be fearful of? Where have your feelings been hurt? Why are you frustrated?

"Lord, grant me the serenity to accept the things I cannot change, the courage to change the things I can, and the wisdom to hide the bodies of those I had to kill because they really hacked me off!"

Anonymous

Have you slowed down enough to interview yourself and take stock of yourself emotionally?

○ Yes
○ No
○ Not sure

Have you shared the results with a close friend?

○ Yes
○ No
○ Not sure

What are the benefits of journaling that make it a "key tool" in the interviewing process?

_____

_____

_____

_____

What role, if any, does it play in your life?

○ Huge
○ Moderate
○ None

Good questions will take us right to the heart of our anger. If we answer them honestly they will help define and clarify the real issue. Is the issue really the trash, or the television or the laundry? What do the issues represent? Is there a fuel dump underneath them, waiting to be ignited?

Interviewing yourself is the only way to take your pulse and decipher the real need.

Wake up and interview your anger!

"If it's neglect that we feel or rejection that we fear, once we unearth those feelings, it becomes possible to deal with them."
Nicole Johnson, Fresh-Brewed Life

What are the main "fuel dumps" in your life?

_____

_____

_____

Where are you in danger of infuriating yourself by "compromising yourself"?

_____

_____

_____

Have you picked up your pen and "written out your heart" in a way that has really led you to deeper meaning and hope?

O   Yes
O   No

Why or why not?

_____

_____

_____

Action Point:

Is there a relationship in your life that was "broken" long ago that has you "limping" today? What can you do to "set it" right?

_____

_____

_____

_____

"It is impossible to live in this world and not be angry, especially if you are searching for hope and love in a world that doesn't have very much to give."

Nicole Johnson, Fresh-Brewed Life

Percolations

Books

* *The Dance of Anger: A Woman's Guide to Changing the Patterns of Intimate Relationships*, Harriet Goldhor Lerner
* *Make Anger your Ally*, Neil Clark Warren
* *Fresh-Brewed Life: A Stirring Invitation to Wake Up Your Soul* (chapter 5)

Movies

* When a Man Loves a Woman
* Dead Man Walking
* The Joy Luck Club
* Prince of Tides

Music

* Lord of the Past: A Compilation, Bob Bennett
* End of Innocence, Don Henley
* Steady On, Shawn Colvin

Fresh-Brewed Adventures

* Take a long walk with your journal. Find a spot along the way to pray. Ask God to show you the areas of your life that cause rage inside you. Listen to what He says and take notes.
* Start an anger log in your journal. Anger is like a submarine: it's hard to track. It stays submerged until something brings it to the surface. Keeping a log of the surfacing will uncover some patterns.
* Write a letter to someone with whom you are angry. Don't have any intention of sending the letter; just use it to clarify some of your feelings. Interview until you find the hurt or the frustration or the fear, and write about that.
* Try exercising the next time you really get angry. Take a time-out and go for a run, get on the stair master, or just walk around the neighborhood twice. You will be amazed how physical exertion can clear your head, release tension, and help you calm down.

Directed Journaling

What is your earliest memory of being angry?

What is your most recent memory of being angry?

Are the two related in any way?

Are you ever dishonest about your anger and hide it?

What are you afraid of?

Notes

_____

_____

_____

_____

_____

_____

_____

_____

_____

_____

Fresh-Brewed Life

Cup Number Four

Change Your World

Reflection and Discussion

MATTHEW 25:24-25

Then he who had received the one talent came and said, 'Lord, I knew you to be a hard man, reaping where you have not sown, and gathering where you have not scattered seed. And I was afraid, and went and hid your talent in the ground. Look, there you have what is yours.'

Change Your World

Creating a fresh-brewed life steaming with significance doesn't just happen. It has to be created. Order doesn't arise out of chaos, order degenerates into chaos. If we simply let our days "run their course," we will find ourselves asleep and missing out on real life in no time. Most of us find it far easier to react to what happens than to take bold steps toward purposefulness.

Think over your life. In all your busyness, how can you make sure you have your priorities in place — things to which you are "purposefully, passionately" committed?

_____

_____

_____

_____

_____

"Character cannot be developed in ease and quiet. Only through experience of trial and suffering can the soul be strengthened, vision cleared, ambition inspired, and success achieved."
Helen Keller

Finding our passion is the single, most important, ingredient in changing our world. A sense of our own gifts and calling is like yeast in bread— giving full, flavor-filled life— without it we just have flat, hard dough.

Uncovering God's purpose in our lives and following it will lead us to the greatest satisfaction there is. When we work out of our God-given passion, we get tired, but not weary. We need rest, but not a change.

How do you pursue your "passion," what Nicole calls "the one thing" without becoming selfish?

_____

_____

_____

_____

_____

Many women don't think in terms of gifts and calling. That's for men. Women just work. Some have even defined God's will as the hardest, worst thing they can think of to do. Bless Jesus. They complain the whole time. There is no joy in their lives; no "change-the-world-spirit," just an angry expectation of brownie points in heaven for taking the hard road. That spirit produces a life that is as stale as two-day old coffee.

"Our deepest fear is not that we are inadequate. Our deepest fear is that we are powerful beyond measure. It is our light, not our darkness, that most frightens us. We ask ourselves, 'Who am I to be brilliant, gorgeous, talented, and famous?' Actually, who are you not to be? You are a child of God."

Nelson Mandela

Is it only a "man's thing" to pursue purpose and significance in life?

○   Yes
○   No
○   Maybe

What does our culture say?

_____

_____

_____

What does God say?

_____

_____

_____

How do you and your friends measure up to Nicole's observation about women who "complete all the tasks but have no joy in the process?"

_____

_____

_____

_____

Relax. Pursuing significance or seeking to change your world doesn't necessarily mean taking on anything new. It might mean doing an analysis of your gifts or getting control of your schedule. This passion that we are looking for is not the "What" so much as it is the "Why." Dream a little. Okay, dream a lot. If you could have any life in the world, whose would it be and why? What is God calling you to do?

"Nothing fails like success because we don't learn from it. We only learn from failure."
Kenneth Boulding

Have your journal open and listen to the Lord, then write down what he tells you.

What are some of the ways that women "postpone their lives" and "put them on hold' by avoiding their passion?

_____

_____

_____

_____

I have a friend who says, "The deepest question of our lives is not 'If you died tonight, do you know where you would spend eternity?' That's a good question and one that must be settled, but an equally deep question is 'If you wake up tomorrow, do you know how you will spend the rest of your life?"

A lot of us aren't afraid of dying. We're afraid of living. We don't know what we are living for. We know that Jesus will be there for us when we die, if we have a relationship with Him, but we are missing the kind of life He is calling us to live today.

Wake up and change your world!

What do you think Nicole means by "changing the world we live in"?

_____

_____

_____

_____

"For most of history, Anonymous was a woman."
Virginia Woolf

Is this happening in your life?

O   Yes
O   No
O   Maybe

Explain.

_____

_____

_____

_____

_____

Discuss how you and your closest friends may pursue this goal more consistently.

_____

_____

_____

_____

_____

"Faith is not making religious sounding noises in the day time. It is asking your innermost self questions at night—and getting up and going to work."
Mary Jean Irion, Yes, World

Percolations

Books

* *The Call: Finding and Fulfilling the Central Purpose of Your Life*,
  Os Guinness
* *Roaring Lambs: A Gentle Plan to Radically Change Your World*, Bob Briner
* *Fresh-Brewed Life: A Stirring Invitation to Wake Up Your Soul* (chapter 8)

Movies

* City Slickers
* The Fisher King
* Awakenings
* Forrest Gump

Music

* Les Miserables, Soundtrack
* Where I Stand, Twila Paris
* Joy in the Journey: Michael Card's Greatest Hits

Fresh-Brewed Adventures

* Get out your good china, wear your favorite blazer, spray your best perfume, and run errands. Have a party with your loved ones because you can. Make a decision to stop postponing your life.

* Try a "Receiving Praise Week." Anytime anyone gives you a compliment, just receive it. No ifs, ands, or buts—just a simple thank-you, period. If any notes of encouragement come your way, take them to a special place, receive them, and thank God for them.

Directed Journaling

* Make a list of phrases that you would love to hear people say about you at your funeral.
* Start thinking about what you want written on your tombstone.
* What gifts has God given you that you aren't using for Him?
* If you wake up tomorrow, will you know what you're living for? What is your passion, your "one thing" that you want your life to be about?

Notes

_____

_____

_____

_____

_____

_____

_____

_____

_____

_____

_____

_____

_____

_____

Conclusion

I haven't finished fresh-brewed life. Even thought our time together is drawing to a close as I write theses last pages, I know I will never be "finished" with this book. Writing about living freshly has served as a more intense wake-up call. I will continue going back over these chapters and drinking from these cups. I encourage you to do the same.

Seeking to stay awake is not a frantic, caffeine-induced alertness, but a consistent, gentle stirring. Keep going back to your whole-bean essence, submitting to being finely ground and allowing God's passion to make the freshest brewed life you can know.

As you get the hang of making a cup, allow God to make a pot. Share a cup of fresh-brewed life. Put enough grounds in the filter to make more than you need. There is a world that desperately needs your fresh-brewed life. Remember, God wastes nothing. Not your sorrows, nor your joys. throw it all in the filter and let Him brew it. Then share a cup with the world.